Run, Reds, Run!

By Cameron Macintosh

Dom is in a run!

Dom is a Red
and Meg is a Red.

Tom is a Red
and Jen is a Red!

Meg runs up to Tom.

Meg has the red rod!

Run, run, run!

As Tom runs,
he gets the rod.

Tom runs up to Dom.

Run, run, run!

Dom runs in the mud!

He tips into it.

Dom gets up!

Dom gets the rod
and runs up to Jen.

Run, run, run!

Jen gets the rod
and runs on.

Jen can see the end.

Jen gets to the end.

CHECKING FOR MEANING

1. Who is the first person to run? *(Literal)*

2. Who does Dom give the rod to? *(Literal)*

3. Why is the relay team called the Reds? *(Inferential)*

EXTENDING VOCABULARY

Dom	Which other word in the story rhymes with *Dom*? Which part of these words is the same?
run	Which letter is different in *ran* and *run*? What words do you know that rhyme with each of these words?
rod	What is a *rod* in this story? What do the runners do with the rod? What is another meaning of this word? Can you use the word *rod* in a sentence where it has a different meaning?

MOVING BEYOND THE TEXT

1. What other relays are there, other than running relays?

2. Does your school have a relay team? What activity do they do?

3. Who do you think is the most important person in a relay? Why?

4. How is participating in a team activity different to an activity you do by yourself?

SPEED SOUNDS

Dd	Jj	Oo	Gg	Uu

Cc	Bb	Rr	Ee	Ff	Hh	Nn

Mm	Ss	Aa	Pp	Ii	Tt

PRACTICE WORDS

Dom

and

run

Red

Meg

Tom

Jen

Reds

runs

red

rod

Run

up

mud

on

gets

end